LIFE IN A
Tundra

by Kari Schuetz

BELLWETHER MEDIA • MINNEAPOLIS, MN

Note to Librarians, Teachers, and Parents:

Blastoff! Readers are carefully developed by literacy experts and combine standards-based content with developmentally appropriate text.

Level 1 provides the most support through repetition of high-frequency words, light text, predictable sentence patterns, and strong visual support.

Level 2 offers early readers a bit more challenge through varied simple sentences, increased text load, and less repetition of high-frequency words.

Level 3 advances early-fluent readers toward fluency through increased text and concept load, less reliance on visuals, longer sentences, and more literary language.

Level 4 builds reading stamina by providing more text per page, increased use of punctuation, greater variation in sentence patterns, and increasingly challenging vocabulary.

Level 5 encourages children to move from "learning to read" to "reading to learn" by providing even more text, varied writing styles, and less familiar topics.

Whichever book is right for your reader, Blastoff! Readers are the perfect books to build confidence and encourage a love of reading that will last a lifetime!

This edition first published in 2016 by Bellwether Media, Inc.

No part of this publication may be reproduced in whole or in part without written permission of the publisher. For information regarding permission, write to Bellwether Media, Inc., Attention: Permissions Department, 5357 Penn Avenue South, Minneapolis, MN 55419.

Library of Congress Cataloging-in-Publication Data

Schuetz, Kari.
  Life in a Tundra / by Kari Schuetz.
     pages cm. – (Blastoff! Readers: Biomes Alive!)
  Summary: "Simple text and full-color photography introduce beginning readers to life in a tundra. Developed by literacy experts for students in kindergarten through third grade"– Provided by publisher.
  Audience: Ages 5-8.
  Audience: K to grade 3.
  Includes bibliographical references and index.
  ISBN 978-1-62617-321-7 (hardcover : alk. paper)
  1. Tundras–Juvenile literature. 2. Tundra ecology–Juvenile literature. I. Title.
  GB571.S47 2016
  577.5'86–dc23
                         2015030764

Text copyright © 2016 by Bellwether Media, Inc. BLASTOFF! READERS and associated logos are trademarks and/or registered trademarks of Bellwether Media, Inc. SCHOLASTIC, CHILDREN'S PRESS, and associated logos are trademarks and/or registered trademarks of Scholastic Inc.

Printed in the United States of America, North Mankato, MN.

Table of Contents

The Tundra Biome

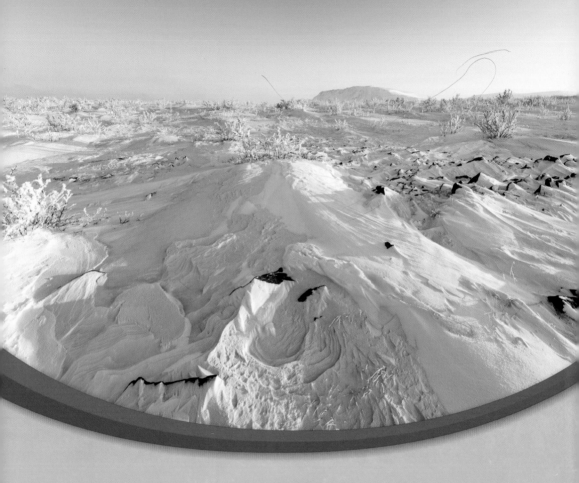

Earth's chilliest **biome** is the tundra. Extreme cold prevents a lot of plant growth.

The tundra is often a desert of ice with no trees. It has a layer of frozen ground called **permafrost**. This never melts!

permafrost

Tundras exist in the **Arctic** and **Antarctic**. These areas receive little sunlight at times. Some winter days have no sunlight at all!

Arctic tundra = ▭   Antarctic tundra = ▭

equator

Tundras are also found at the top of cold mountain ranges. Up high, it is too chilly and windy for much to grow.

The Climate

Canadian
tundra

The tundra **climate** is most known for long, dark winters. Little **precipitation** falls there.

Temperatures can stay below **freezing** for up to ten months a year. Strong winds make temperatures feel even colder.

Alaskan tundra

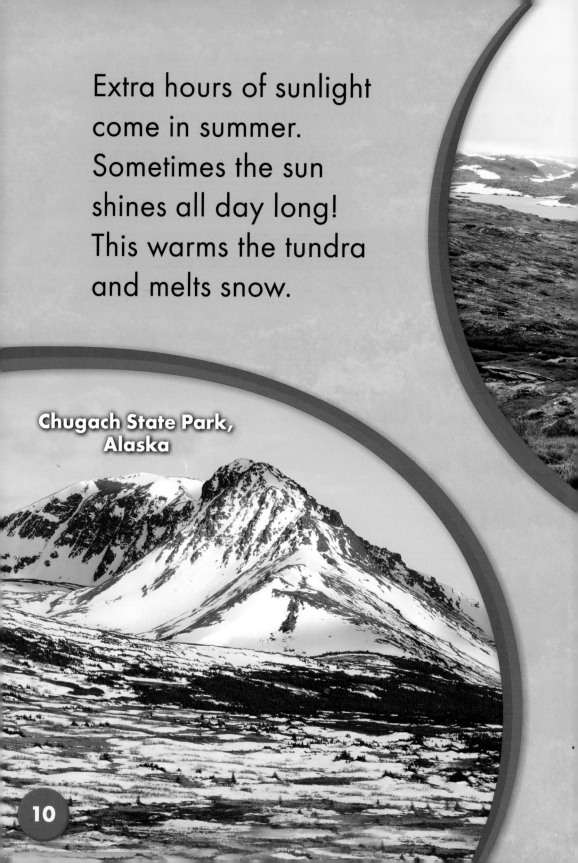

Extra hours of sunlight come in summer. Sometimes the sun shines all day long! This warms the tundra and melts snow.

Chugach State Park, Alaska

Norwegian tundra

Melted snow cannot drain through permafrost. Pools of water form on the land's surface. They refreeze when colder weather returns.

The Plants

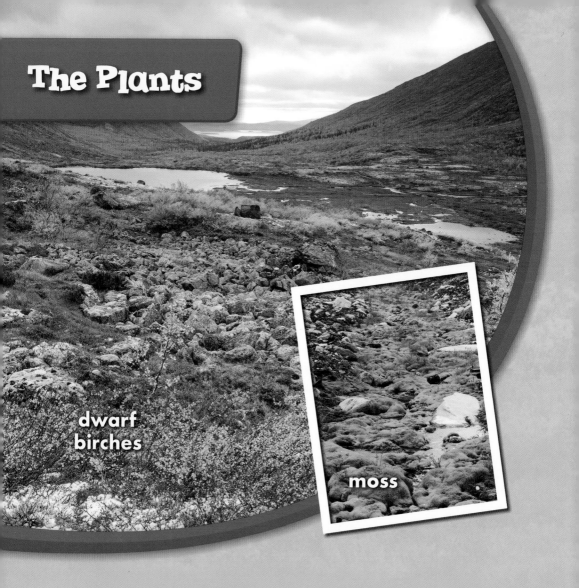

dwarf birches

moss

Only **shrubs** and other small plants grow in the tundra. They stay low to the ground and close together to avoid strong, cold winds.

Plant **roots** stay near the surface. They cannot grow through permafrost.

Arctic willow

Tundra plants live with little water and sunlight. They can grow under snow!

bearberries

pasqueflowers

Plant leaves are small to limit water loss. In summer, flowering plants bloom quickly.

15

The Animals

Canada geese and snow geese migrating

polar bear

Tundra animals have ways to survive the winter. Some **hibernate** during the extreme cold. Most birds **migrate** to warmer climates.

Many animals grow thick fur and gain fat for warmth. Some have white coloring to blend in with snow. This helps them hunt or hide.

snowshoe hare

snowy owl

Animals are active in the summer. They drink from the pools of melted snow. Some animals eat plants and insects.

reindeer

Arctic fox

Other animals hunt. They eat
a lot to store up fat for the
long winter!

The Baffin Coastal Tundra

Location: Nunavut, Canada;
north-central coast of Baffin Island

Baffin Island

Baffin
Costal Tundra

N
W   E
S

Size: 3,500 square miles
(9,065 square kilometers)

Temperature:

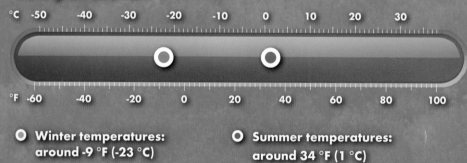

°C	-50	-40	-30	-20	-10	0	10	20	30

°F	-60	-40	-20	0	20	40	60	80	100

○ Winter temperatures:
around -9 °F (-23 °C)

○ Summer temperatures:
around 34 °F (1 °C)

Precipitation: 8 to 12 inches
(20 to 30 centimeters) per year

BAFFIN COASTAL TUNDRA FOOD WEB

rock ptarmigan

Arctic fox

Arctic hare

lemming

Arctic willow

moss

Other important plants: sedges, Arctic poppies, dryas, purple saxifrage

Other important animals: polar bears, caribou, northern fulmars, snow buntings

Glossary

Antarctic—the cold region around the South Pole

Arctic—the cold region around the North Pole

biome—a nature community defined by its climate, land features, and living things

climate—the specific weather conditions for an area

freezing—32 degrees Fahrenheit (0 degrees Celsius); the temperature at which water freezes into ice.

hibernate—to sleep or rest through the winter

migrate—to travel from one place to another, often with the seasons

permafrost—a layer of tundra ground that always stays frozen

precipitation—water that falls to the earth from the sky

roots—the underground parts of a plant; roots hold a plant in place and take in water.

shrubs—short, woody plants

To Learn More

AT THE LIBRARY

Amstutz, Lisa J. *Polar Animal Adaptations*. Mankato, Minn.: Capstone Press, 2012.

Labrecque, Ellen. *Arctic Tundra*. Chicago, Ill.: Heinemann Library, 2014.

Slade, Suzanne. *What If There Were No Lemmings? A Book About the Tundra Ecosystem*. Mankato, Minn.: Picture Window Books, 2011.

ON THE WEB
Learning more about tundras is as easy as 1, 2, 3.

1. Go to www.factsurfer.com.

2. Enter "tundras" into the search box.

3. Click the "Surf" button and you will see a list of related web sites.

With factsurfer.com, finding more information is just a click away.

Index

The images in this book are reproduced through the courtesy of: Jim H Walling, front cover (owl); Alaska Stock/ Corbis, front cover (caribou); Sergei Drozd, front cover (background); Nordroden, p. 4; Wildlife GmbH/ Alamy, p. 5; Theo Allofs/ Corbis, p. 8; AccentAlaska.com/ Alamy, p. 9; Jonathan Nafzger, p. 10; Brykaylo Yuriy, p. 11; Gregory A. Pozhvanov, p. 12 (left); Natalia Davidovich, p. 12 (right); Alexander Piragis, p. 13; tbkmedia de/ Alamy, p. 14; Natallia Khlapushyna/ Alamy, p. 15; Sylvie Bouchard, p. 16 (left); AndreAnita, p. 16 (right); MVPhoto, p. 17 (left); Critterbiz, p. 17 (right); Meekeetza, p. 18; Arterra Picture Library/ Alamy, p. 19; Egmont Strigl/ Glow Images, p. 20; bozulek, p. 21 (Arctic fox); Tatiana Ivkovich, p. 21 (rock ptarmigan); Dan Bach Kristensen, p. 21 (Arctic hare); tobiasjo, p. 21 (lemming); Alexander Piragis, p. 21 (Arctic willow); Vladimir Melnik, p. 21 (moss).